End

Power Up is a must read. Pastor Jamie Tuttle beautifully articulates how to activate your purpose. So many are looking and longing for their purpose to be revealed. This book has your answer! Buckle up and let's GROW!

Real Talk Kim Jones
Author, Speaker

If anyone has the authority to write on Kingdom purpose, it is Pastor Jamie Tuttle. I have personally known Jamie for over two decades and have watched him live out God's plan for his life. Your purpose is decided by God, but it must be discovered by you. In his latest book, *Power Up*, Pastor Jamie will take you on a journey to discover yours.

Dr. Dave Martin
Speaker and Best-Selling Author

My friend, Jamie Tuttle, and his family have been tremendous blessings in my life for many years. His life is a testimony to the power of expectant prayer, and his ability to teach others the strategies of receiving answers to prayer and activating their purpose is manifest throughout the entirety of this book. Jamie has done a masterful job of demonstrating how to live a life full of holiness and devoid of compromise; you'll be equipped to aggressively claim and reclaim enemy held territory for the Kingdom of God in your sphere of influence.

Rod Parsley
Founder & Lead Pastor
World Harvest Church

My friend, Pastor Jamie Tuttle, has heard from Heaven and I'm thrilled to see him put those words to paper for all to read! Beyond simply being inspired and challenged, this book will cause you to fulfill its title. You will power UP to your God given destiny!

Tony Suarez
Revivalmakers Ministries

My friend, Jamie Tuttle, has written a great book on activating our purpose. Read this, open your heart and get ready to be challenged, empowered and prepared for your next level!

Jim Raley
Calvary Christian Center
Ormond Beach, FL

In his book, *Power Up*, Pastor Jamie Tuttle makes clear what the Kingdom assignment is for the Church. Get ready to be commissioned into the most powerful season of your life!

Darryl Strawberry
MLB Baseball Great, Inspirational Speaker

POWER UP

Activating the
Purpose of God
in Your Life

POWER UP

Activating the
Purpose of God
in Your Life

JAMIE TUTTLE

hsp
HIS SONG
PUBLISHING

Visit Pastor Jamie's website at JamieTuttle.org for Biblical resources that will equip and empower you to walk in the miracle-working power of the Holy Spirit. You can also subscribe to his podcast, *PowerWords with Jamie Tuttle*, on iTunes or Spotify.

Cover design by Joe Potter
www.joepotter.com or www.graphiks.com

Photography by Erica Tuttle

Published by His Song Publishing

ISBN: 978-0-578-39492-3 (Paperback)

Religion / Christian Living / General
Religion / Christian Living / Spiritual Growth
Religion / Christian Living / Prayer

TABLE OF CONTENTS

Acknowledgements

This book is very special to me and is simply a dream come true. I am so grateful for those who have supported and participated in this effort.

To my wife, Judy Jacobs, your encouragement, support, and "It's in you to do this, Jamie," has been who you are to me for over 29 years. Everything we've ever done, we've done it together, and I wouldn't change a thing. I love you!

To my daughters, Kaylee and Erica, you are my world. Every day you teach me the importance of being a great leader, listener, and loving dad.

To the greatest staff and ministry team ever, every day you run with vision—some written down, some not. Your heart and passion for God and His Kingdom constantly impacts the world.

To Minister Jamie Rohrbaugh, and From His Presence Ministry, your unbelievable efforts and impact to this vision will never go unnoticed. You are such an encourager, Christlike example, and strong vessel, building His Kingdom every day. Thank you for seeing beyond the Message.

To Holly and Timothy VonWald, and your relentless

commitment to excellence. Wow! You bring new meaning to being "just a phone call away." The fact that I hold this book in my hand is a miracle.

To my Dwelling Place family, every week, you listen, you respond, you worship and praise God for who He is and what He's doing in our midst. What an incredible body of believers you are! We are in this together.

To my Heavenly Father, You called me and placed Your purpose in me. Your constant vision drives me to go higher, deeper, and wider all at the same time. My heart's desire is and always will be You.

Foreword

In his book, *Power Up: Activating the Purpose of God in Your Life*, Jamie Tuttle—my husband—has given us the tools to walk in Power, Anointing, Authority, and Boldness!

In a day when it seems that we are living in a culture that is spineless, silent, and politically correct, Jamie is calling us out as the Church to become what God has ordained for us to be in this world.

It's time for us to stand up and be proactive in winning the lost, in changing our culture to look more like Jesus, and in walking in the power of "His Might."

The Bible says in Daniel 11:32, *"the people who know their God shall be strong, and carry out great exploits."*

That's YOU and ME! I know that, as you read this *powerful* word, it will stir and move you to *Power Up* in His Strength! Let's go! It's time to roar!

Judy Jacobs
Author & Speaker

PART 1

COMMISSIONED TO ROAR

CHAPTER 1

PRAYING AND DECLARING POWER INTO YOUR LIFE

My friend, are you ready for a spiritual power infusion today?

God has been moving radically in churches across Tennessee, where I pastor. The thundering revival we are experiencing here is fueled by PRAYER. Here at *Dwelling Place Church International*, we are actively engaged in aggressive prayer—unceasing prayer with dedicated prayer meetings multiple days per week, activating our intercessors, and combining fasting with prayer. God is moving because our people are praying.

I believe He wants to do the same for you. The same way we are seeing the Lord move in household salvations, healings, financial breakthroughs, deliverances, and more, God can and will do the same for you if you will pray.

Many people tell us that they don't know how to pray, and I understand that. So, I wanted to help you today by providing a sample prayer, showing the way I am leading my congregation to pray here in the Tennessee Revival.

If you're at a loss for how to begin praying with power—how to begin praying prayers that move Heaven and shake the earth—then the prayer below will help you get started. Use it as a framework, but let the Spirit of the Lord lead you to pray His words back to Him as He flows through *your* spirit.

Are you ready? Pray this prayer and declaration over yourself and your house today:

> *"Heavenly Father, we come to You in Jesus' name. We bless Your name, Jesus. We honor You. We lift You up, Lord. You are worthy of all the glory and the honor.*
>
> *Lord, thank You for miracles. Thank You for healing. Thank You, Lord, for opening doors for me. Thank You for making a way where there was no way. Thank You for increase. Thank You for Your fresh outpouring on me today; for Your fresh anointing; for the fresh manifestation of Your presence. Thank You, Lord, that what the enemy meant for bad, You have turned around for my good.*
>
> *Hallelujah! I magnify Your name, Lord. I join my praises with those of the angels and with the great cloud of witnesses right now, Lord, and we exalt Your name together. There's nobody like You, Lord.*
>
> *Lord, Your presence is heaven in this room. You have a plan; You have a purpose; You have a design.*
>
> *Lord, right now in my life, I choose to receive. I open up my heart, mind, and soul to receive Your Word.*

You never disappoint; never. You never let us down. You are the same yesterday, today, and forever—and You promise to be the same forever. Thank You, Lord.

Father, thank You that there is healing in this room where I am right now, for You are here. There's encouragement in this room. There are open doors in this room, and it's all available to me right now by Your Spirit.

Thank You, God, that You move on the wings of my worship and praise.

Your prophetic Spirit and Word are in the room with me and in my heart right now.

Your declared Word is right here with me and in me today, Lord, and I thank You. Sweet Holy Spirit, precious Lord, do everything in me today that You want to do, in Jesus' name.

Father, in Jesus' name, I unify and come together in one accord with Your Spirit, Your Word, and Your Body, and I agree and declare with them in one accord You are all- powerful, all-knowing, and You're present everywhere. I confess and agree with Your Spirit that anything is possible right now. Anything is possible for me today, for I am with You and You are in me.

Lord, I choose to go to the next level in my prayer and in worship today.

I agree with Your Word that no weapon formed against me or my family shall be able to prosper, and any tongue that should try to bring us down shall prove to be in the wrong.

Lord, Your presence is in me. Your Spirit is in me. You have manifest Yourself in this room where I am, right now. And Lord, I boldly confess and declare that:

- *No accusation shall stand in the presence of God.*
- *No lie will stand in the presence of God.*
- *No evil spirit shall be able to stand in the presence of God; Your presence casts out all evil.*

Father, I thank You that perfect peace belongs to me, for my heart and mind are stayed on You. I thank You:

- *that testimonies reside and resound in this house;*
- *that something new is taking place;*
- *that something new is pressing forth;*
- *that something new is coming out;*
- *that something new is coming forward for me right now.*

I thank You that the dark days are over, and the days of light are at hand for me and all the individuals in my house.

I thank You, God, that the promises of the Lord Almighty are yes and amen. I thank You today that healing is the children's bread; it is my bread, for I am Your child. I thank You that the enemy is destroyed and exposed right now, today, in Your presence.

Lord, I thank You that the enemy is exposed. I say right now that any false spirit and any lies of the devil are exposed by the light and anointing of the Spirit of Almighty God today.

I thank You, God, that You not only hear prayer, but that You answer prayer.

I thank You today that You are moving among Your people and in my life. I thank You today that the anointing of Your Holy Ghost is moving right now in my life by the prayer of agreement. I thank You that the prayer of faith is moving in my life right now as well, and that You are saturating my heart, moving in my home, and moving in my life.

Lord, I confess and boldly declare that You are restoring that which the enemy destroyed. You're bringing back lost souls in my family, church, and neighborhood. You're bringing unhappy people to Yourself and are making them happy with the joy of the Lord today.

I thank You today, God, that the joy of the Lord is

our strength. I thank You that the blessing of the Lord makes us rich, and You add no sorrow to it. Hallelujah!

I am Your child, Father God, and my family belongs to you. My church, city, and nation belong to you. And I declare and decree that we are the people of God and we are free; and whom the Son sets free is free indeed."

Hallelujah! If you prayed that prayer, don't stop there! Stay in the attitude of prayer, praise, and worship, and clap your hands unto the Lord! Shout unto God with a voice of triumph!

My friend, no matter what's going on in your life, PRAYER has never been more important.

We're seeing God move across our great state of Tennessee because God's people are *praying*. God's move isn't limited to a church in Tennessee, though.

Wherever you are, and no matter what your life looks like, I urge you to become a man or woman of prayer:

- Pray the prayer above right now, but don't stop praying.
- Pray in the Spirit wherever you go.
- Pray in English.
- Pray in the language of your homeland.

Whatever you do, now more than ever, I urge you to STAY before the throne of grace in a bold position of prayer. If you will do so, just as we have been seeing amazing miracles both at *Dwelling Place Church* and across the state of Tennessee, you also will obtain a constant river of mercy and grace to help in your time of need.

CHAPTER 2

CAN YOU HEAR THE BREAKTHROUGH?

"... for it is God who works in you both to will and to do for His good pleasure."
Philippians 2:13

Have you been praying for breakthrough, with no apparent results? Do you feel like God isn't moving in your life anymore? Are you wondering what happened to the powerful move of the Spirit you used to enjoy?

It's vitally important for you to understand today that God's movement in your life is not a one-time thing. God wants to do something powerful for you every day. He is all the while effectively at work, both to will and to do His good pleasure.

God is active in your life right now.

He doesn't take time off. He doesn't take Passover, Resurrection Sunday, or Pentecost off; He neither slumbers nor sleeps. He is moving *right now*; He is currently active and at work on your behalf. He is in all things, of all things, and creating all things—and He never stops. That's who He is; He's a massive God with massive power, and He is currently involved in *everything* that concerns you.

The Lord wants you to know today that He has already gone ahead of you in your planned destination. He already IS where you think you're going. He has already made a way where you don't think there is any way at all. Someone reading this has been waiting for the way to come into existence, but you need to know that God is already there. He does not rest, and He is actively at work in your prayer life.

God is actively at work on your prayer list right now.

He is actively and *all the while* working on the things that you don't even know to pray yet. He is already working on things that you haven't thought of yet. He sees your tomorrow, and He goes ahead and begins working and performing His miracles in the future of your life—long before you arrive in that future. *God is all the while working miracles before you arrive at the place of the miracle.*

And the Bible says that you have an enemy—but that enemy can't stop your breakthrough.

When the Philistines heard that David had been anointed King of Israel, they planned and strategized to fight and capture him. In the same way, your enemy is listening to what's happening in your life right now.

Anytime that you have been positioned or anointed for greatness, the enemy listens for your anointing to be announced. He prepares, plans, and strategizes. He says, "My assignment is to prevent that from happening." Your enemy wants to bring turmoil, testing, stress, and struggle. "It is my assignment," the enemy says, "to keep you—the anointed one, the one called by God, appointed by God, anointed by God—from your greatness. I have an assignment to stop."

That's why you feel like you're fighting everything right now.

That's why you feel like you're up against everything right now. That's why you're dreaming bad dreams right now. That's why you're having health struggles right now. That's why it feels like you can't make ends meet financially right now. It's all because the devil has heard you're anointed, and he has determined to get in the way of what God is doing in your life.

Your enemy comes to steal, kill, and destroy. He disguises himself in bad health, family issues, and workplace problems. He disguises himself in accusation and bad attitudes.

Nevertheless, Jesus said, "Don't fear that. I have overcome the world. I am more powerful and more anointed. I have called you out."

Since God anointed and crowned you, the enemy has no power to prevent what God is doing to do in your life.

Sometimes we make our situations bigger than we make the God who lives in us. We magnify the problem. But, God has anointed you to be great for Him. He's a massive God who makes even the biggest problem look insignificant. If you will keep your eyes and ears trained on Him, you will hear your breakthrough coming and nothing will hinder it.

CHAPTER 3

WHY WE NEED TO ROAR

My heart is burning. Friend, we are not in a gather-round-the-sofa, 30-minute-family-sitcom, caramel-apple-eating moment in the Church. We are not in a time of peace and safety. Instead, we are at war with the devil—at war with those who are sold out to him!

The enemy has created a divide between believers of all races, backgrounds, and stories.

The truth is that our predetermined differences are what make us, as God's people, so great. But instead of embracing what could be the strength of our diversity, we are fighting each other. Meanwhile, right before our eyes, the enemy is taking our territory.

We in the Church have given way to a "temper tantrum, fatherless, give-me-what's-mine, I-deserve-it" culture, but we are supposed to be the strong ones who walk in freedom! Nevertheless, most of us aren't strong or free enough to get through the day without attacking our brothers and sisters in Christ over their choice of political candidates—or even over things like clothing, body weight, appearances, opinions, history, failures, jealousy, and anything else destructive that we can find.

Then, spending all this time creating division and tearing people down, we ask God to bless us beyond measure. This is not the Kingdom of God, nor is it the reason Christ died.

Deuteronomy 28 teaches us about both the blessings of God and the curses of God, based on His covenant. If we choose to do the works of God, we will be exponentially blessed! However, if we choose to do the works of the devil, we will be cursed.

First John 3:8 says, "Jesus came to DESTROY the works of the devil."

We are supposed to be completely out of agreement with the devil and all his works. Like Jesus, we are only to do what the Father does and say what the Father says. However, in many cases, we have allowed sin of all kinds to become the new "normal" instead. We have embraced and even come to revere the doctrines of darkness, based on trash propaganda and a lazy refusal to study, understand, and interpret the Bible.

It's as if the Church has crawled into bed and fallen asleep under the covers—while all of hell celebrates the fact that the Church forfeited the game.

We've accepted the lots assigned to us by corrupt, anti-Christ government leaders. We have completely forgotten what we are and who we have confessed ourselves to be through Jesus Christ. Church, we must stop this craziness. We have got to wake up before it's too late!

One of my dear Bishop friends and mentors, a godly man in his 80s from one of our great inner cities in the northern US, said to me recently, "Jamie, those who claim to be godly, yet are married to politics, sinful natures, behaviors, and fighting over various parts of our history, are dressed in the armor of flesh. They will fall to destruction."

He continued by saying this: "I've pastored most of my life. I've raised up sons and daughters for Kingdom service, and I've seen literally hundreds of thousands of people saved and healed. But, I've never seen a time when people are so cold toward each other and are even turning on what they know and believe. We need a *Presence of God* awakening in America."

His words cut through me like a knife because he described the things that are festering in the Body of Christ perfectly.

The enemy—through evil people, strategies, and witchcraft—has turned us on each other:

- We are killing our own wounded.
- We are joining with the forces that hide truth and funnel lies.
- We are coming into agreement with people who make public anti-God, anti-Christ, and anti-Church statements.

Meanwhile, at the same time, these agents of darkness patronize us as if we are their puppets on a string. Then, we have the audacity to get excited over our false "inclusivity."

As I am writing this, we are in a particularly divisive time in the United States where I live. Many of the current conflicts are driven by Satanic occultism, New Age theology, and many other evil practices.

And it's not just the country that's divided. Unfortunately, division is keeping us—the Church—weak too, while it makes the people who cause the division strong. It gives them control, for to be divisive is to be powerful. Yet, all the while, few people seem to take Biblical ethics and real, foundational convictions to the voting booth. This means that we, as Christians, are too often voting for anyone who says they will give us what we want, to satisfy our fleshly desires.

But in all of this, we forget what is good for the Kingdom of God and its establishment in the earth.

The end result is that:

- people stay angry;
- pastors are ridiculed for preaching truth, or for not saying the truth 'just right';
- churches are emptied;
- families are separated;
- friendships are broken...

...and such cycles have continued for generations.

It's sad, but so many people shamelessly agree with the strategies of darkness. They turn the other way and never take an openly biblical stance against obvious evil. Then I hear, "Well, the Church shouldn't get involved in politics and in the affairs of America. Stay in your lane; call a prayer meeting; raise the tithe; sing a worship song; and let that be it. Let the rest of them figure it out."

People say these things despite the fact that Daniel, the assistant to the king, was called upon to:

- announce what God said for the nation;
- interpret dreams;
- bring correction to sin; and
- expose dark corruption.

We also seem to have forgotten that Queen Esther was picked out, chosen by God, and positioned with great favor in the king's quarters to defend God's people and make sure righteousness and justice for Israel were established. Also, what about the prophet Samuel, God's man, who anointed young David to be the greatest king of Israel? God led Samuel to anoint David specifically so David could:

- lead the nation in uninhibited worship;
- prepare the nation for God's presence;
- defeat the enemies of God; and
- bring glory to the name of God.

God expects His Church to be His voice in the earth, PERIOD.

The Church must take its rightful place at this time as the apostolic gatekeeper of the whole world. If we do not, then we fail our assignment to bring redemption to the world through Christ's death on the cross.

We all deserve judgment for our sin.

There's no such thing as "survival in the end" without the blood of Jesus on our hearts, and that blood, when applied, changes everything about us. The blood of Jesus delivers us, sets us free, empowers us, keeps us in our right mind, fights our every battle, goes before us, goes behind us, goes beside us, keeps us covered, speaks for us when we are wronged, and ultimately cleanses us for all wickedness. The blood of Jesus does all of those things for us and more—and it never compromises.

Let me say that again.

The blood of Jesus was poured out for you, and it never compromises, nor will it ever endorse any compromise you or I make.

Jesus died to do away with sin completely. He died to annihilate the works of the devil. And His blood stands for something: the TRUTH—for Jesus is the Way, the Truth, and the Life. If you name the name of Christ as your Savior, then you cannot make the choice to flee away from the blood of Jesus, the truth He is, and the holiness for which He died.

My friend, we are in a war. The Church must stand against evil of every kind in this hour. We must stand in our survival gear—that of Jesus' blood, His Word, His name, and the unchanging unity and love of Kingdom brothers and sisters.

The blood of Jesus, and the truth of His Word, will transcend time and eternity. It will collect those who name Jesus as Lord, and eventually it will judge those who embrace darkness rather than light.

There are only two options available to every individual. We're either in the Kingdom of God, agreeing with and obeying the truth of His Word, or we're not.

At the end of the day, like Moses, we must ask, "Who is on the Lord's side?"

And if we in the Church are not convicted about what we have become and about what we have allowed in this nation, then the words "I'm saved" are just motivational affirmations with neither fruit nor truth—and we have never really had a true heart conversion.

However:

- If your spirit leaps, excitement explodes within you, and you become filled with righteous indignation over the sin in our land;

- If your spirit eyes open and burn with fire like the eyes of Christ do;

- If you're driven by the power of revival, and not by what's popular;

- And if you truly believe what God says—that righteousness exalts a nation—and if you reject the ridiculous behavior of culture and mankind...

Then wherever you are, shout out today into this great country:

"Salvation belongs to our God! And because of the blood of His Son, I am saved and I am not ashamed!"

Church, it's time to roar the call of righteousness over our land. It's time to wake up before it's too late. If we won't roar, then who will?

CHAPTER 4

THE ROAR STARTS WITH YOU

My friend, we can talk about rising up all we want, but the fact of the matter is that the "roar" starts with YOU.

It starts with me, too. It starts with my wife and family. My point is, the roar starts with each of us. We *each* have to take individual responsibility to burn for Christ. We *each* have to take personal responsibility to burn for holiness. We *each* have to decide to cling to Christ and relentlessly seek Him, standing on His Word and obeying it. Then, in the face of an opposing culture, we each must stand up with a voice and Kingdom aggression and proclaim, in the words traditionally ascribed to Martin Luther, *"Here I stand; I can do no other."*

I have done this. I have taken this stand, and I'm not turning back. I have dedicated my whole life to the preaching of the Gospel, and my quest to glorify Christ and make disciples of all nations will never end.

What about you?

The entire focus of this book is to commission you to walk in

POWER. My intention with everything written here is to charge you, inspire you, adjure you, and equip you *in the name of Jesus* to stand up, power up, and go out to aggressively dominate and rule for Jesus in your domain. Wherever the Lord has called you to be; whomever He has called you to disciple; whatever He has called you to do—*do it with power for the glory of God, and to advance His Kingdom.*

But this kind of Kingdom aggression takes commitment. After you begin, there's no turning back. Jesus taught us this in Luke 9:57-62, which says:

> *Now it happened as they journeyed on the road, that someone said to Him, "Lord, I will follow You wherever You go." And Jesus said to him, "Foxes have holes and birds of the air have nests, but the Son of Man has nowhere to lay His head." Then He said to another, "Follow Me." But he said, "Lord, let me first go and bury my father." Jesus said to him, "Let the dead bury their own*
>
> *dead, but you go and preach the kingdom of God." And another also said, "Lord, I will follow You, but let me first go and bid them farewell who are at my house." But Jesus said to him, "No one, having put his hand to the plow, and looking back, is fit for the kingdom of God."*

The good news is that there's GRACE for your journey. God Himself, who lives in you, will empower you along the way to do everything He desires for you to do. His sweet Holy Spirit—the Comforter, Helper, and Enabler—is your secret source of power, and He wants to do mighty exploits through you. He truly wants you to dominate and rule in whatever your domain or sphere of influence is.

But you're going to have to be aggressive in order to power up and conquer. Jesus has already won the victory, but you're going to have to walk like a victor, talk like a victor, and *act* like a victor in every area in order to experience His power in your life. If you don't embrace His power and His Spirit, letting Him flow through your body, soul, and spirit to accomplish His work on the earth, then nothing will get done. If you don't embrace His mighty call on your life, which can and will be fulfilled if you listen and heed His Holy Spirit, then you'll live your life without ever doing the greater works Jesus said you could do.

Will you choose to be aggressive in your pursuit of Jesus, His Kingdom, and His righteousness today? Will you live for Christ and pursue holiness, without which no one shall see the Lord (Hebrews 12:14)?

In Matthew 11:12, Jesus said:

> *"And from the days of John the Baptist until now the kingdom of heaven suffers violence, and the violent take it by force."*

In this book, I am calling you to be one of the powerful ones—one of the spiritually-violent ones. In the name of Jesus, I am inviting you to rise up, power up, and charge forward with a roar of advancement for His Kingdom.

Will you do this? Do you want this? Will you be an advancer

of the Kingdom, both in your life and everywhere on planet Earth the Father may send you?

If you will, I invite you to commit! Sign your name and write the date below in response to this statement of commitment.

ON THIS DAY, I COMMIT

On this day, I commit my life to become relentless in my pursuit of Jesus Christ and His Kingdom. By the Spirit of God, the grace of God, and the power of His might within me, I will be an aggressive advancer of the will of God on the earth from this day forward.

_____   ___/___/____

Name   Date

PART 2

COMMISSIONED TO ADVANCE

INTRODUCTION

"For unto us a Child is born, unto us a Son is given; and the government will be upon His shoulder. And His name will be called Wonderful, Counselor, Mighty God, Everlasting Father, Prince of Peace. Of the increase of His government and peace there will be no end, upon the throne of David and over His kingdom, to order it and establish it with judgment and justice from that time forward, even forever. The zeal of the Lord of hosts will perform this."
Isaiah 9:6-7 NKJV

We're not in the same old same old anymore.

The people of God are not doing life as usual anymore. God is moving in a radical way in His church. He's speaking loudly and getting His people ready for Jesus to return.

No man knows the day or the hour when Jesus will come back. However, I will say this. Nearly every prophetic word in Scripture has been fulfilled. I believe the Messiah is probably saddling up His white horse right now, knowing that our Father is going to give the cue soon. I believe the angels are preparing for Jesus to depart Heaven's edge, come to this earth, and establish the Kingdom of Heaven in the earth.

If we want to track with the Lord's agenda in this hour, it's time for you and me to become just as aggressive about advancing His Kingdom as He is.

In this section of this book, I'm going to challenge you. I'm going to show you how God has *already* commissioned you to advance His Kingdom—and HOW you can do that.

Are you ready? Saddle your horse; put on your running shoes; start your engines. However you want to get ready, just get ready QUICKLY…because Jesus is coming, and He needs YOU on His advance strategy team.

CHAPTER 5

YOUR ADVANCEMENT ASSIGNMENT

"And from the time John the Baptist began preaching until now, the Kingdom of Heaven has been forcefully advancing, and violent people are attacking it."
Matthew 11:12 NLT

Matthew 11:12 tells us that the Kingdom of Heaven is not standing still. It is forcefully advancing, and the violent are taking it by force.

The violence mentioned here is not sinful violence, like rioting or vandalism. The violence the Bible is talking about means that the people who are members of Jesus' Body— those who are part of the Kingdom—are taking that Kingdom by force. In short, there is a powerful army establishing and expanding the Kingdom of God.

You have an assignment.

You have an individual assignment AND you are part of an army of people with an assignment. You have a commission on the earth to do something with the Kingdom of Heaven backing you. Your commission is to bring the Kingdom of Heaven into the earth. It is to establish the Kingdom of Heaven in the earth.

There's more to your assignment than a 9- to-5 job, a dog named Ralph, and a husband or wife that keeps you company at night. There's more to your assignment than mowing the lawn, doing the laundry, or taking the kids to after-school sports.

Have you ever wondered what your assignment is? Have you ever thought about what your gifting represents? The answer is simple. You have a single mandate from God:

Establish the Kingdom of Heaven on the earth.

Make the earth look just like Heaven. Turn the whole earth into the Embassy of Heaven with YOU as Heaven's ambassador.

You are assigned to establish godly principles right here and right now—wherever you are. If you do not know that, then you will wonder and wander in a domain that you are supposed to dominate.

You are not merely supposed to exist. Your assignment is to be aggressive; to dominate earth's domain.

It's just like formal education. After you graduate from high school—even if you were a champion there—you aren't allowed to stay there. You have to move on to the next place, forcefully advancing into the college realm. You're supposed to take your giftings and anointings, go to college, and learn how to dominate in that new sphere.

Your Kingdom assignment works the same way. Your commission is to dominate where you are; then, after you dominate in that place, move on and dominate the next thing too. Do this over and over until you have taken the whole earth for Christ.

So today, ask the Lord to show you in what areas you have become complacent with occupying the domain instead of dominating it. Ask Him to shake you up and make you hungry for more. Ask Him to help you start down the path of actually fulfilling your assignment on the earth—without hesitating, without regrets, and with BOLD faith.

CHAPTER 6

WALK IN YOUR AUTHORITY

"Then the seventh angel sounded: And there were loud voices in heaven, saying, "The kingdoms of this world have become the kingdoms of our Lord and of His Christ, and He shall reign forever and ever!"
Revelation 11:15 NKJV

It's vitally important that you understand that you are not part of the kingdom of this world. If you think you're a part of the kingdom of this world, you've bought the wrong bill of goods.

The truth is that you are a supernatural being in a natural habitat. Your purpose is divine.

"Divine" means "God-connected." A "divine" thing is connected to God's likeness, His person, and His place.

You are part of the divine makeup of God's Kingdom in Heaven. You are filled with supernatural authority. Your authority doesn't come through a man. It doesn't come through a government. It doesn't come through an ID badge somebody delivered to you in the mail. It doesn't come through your mama and it doesn't come through your earthly daddy. Your authority doesn't come from who you say you are or even from who you believe you are.

No, your authority comes from Heaven above. It comes down to Earth to you and fills you up—just like it fills everyone who says, "I want God more than I want anything else."

According to Webster's Dictionary, a "kingdom" can be several things:[1]

First of all, it's "a politically organized community or major territorial unit having a monarchical form of government headed by a king or queen."

When I read that definition, I think of England, Scotland, and Wales—the United Kingdom. I think of various countries in Europe that still have monarchies. I think of Parliament, of Queen Elizabeth, and of Prince William and Prince Harry.

But where I live, in the United States of America, we don't always "get" the idea of "kingdom" because our government is not set up in the terms of a kingdom domain. Nevertheless, God's Word says that HIS domain is expressed as a Kingdom. Heaven manifests on the earth as a Kingdom—the Kingdom of heaven. That's why Jesus prayed, "Your Kingdom come, Your will be done on earth as it is in Heaven."

What does this mean? It means that our job is to say this to the Father:

"Lord, whatever You're doing in Heaven, we're giving you

---

[1] https://www.merriam-webster.com/dictionary/kingdom
accessed on November 24, 2020

permission to do here on the earth too."

We are supposed to stand on the earth in the authority of Heaven and petition the Father to do here on Earth *exactly* what He's doing in Heaven.

What would this earth look like if we all did just that? How would *your* life look different if everything about you, your life, and your family looked just like Heaven?

I think we should find out, don't you?

Your assignment today is to look at your life and ask the Lord to show you which part to work on TODAY. Ask Him to reveal to you what that aspect of your life would look like if this were Heaven. Then, get started on making the changes He shows you to make. It's just that simple.

CHAPTER 7

DOMINATE THROUGH YOUR PRAYERS

"Let us therefore come boldly to the throne of grace, that
we may obtain mercy and find grace
to help in time of need."
Hebrews 4:16 NKJV

You are the Lord's heavenly being placed here on the earth. And as we have already discussed, your assignment is to make the earth look just like Heaven.

In Matthew 6:9-13, Jesus taught the disciples to pray like this:

> *"In this manner, therefore, pray: 'Our Father in heaven, hallowed be Your name. Your kingdom come. Your will be done on earth as it is in heaven. Give us this day our daily bread. And forgive us our debts, as we forgive our debtors. And do not lead us into temptation, but deliver us from the evil one. For Yours is the kingdom and the power and the glory forever. Amen." Matthew 6:9-13 NKJV*

In other words, Jesus instructed the disciples to pray, *"Lord, whatever You're doing there, do here too. Also, feed us on earth what You're serving up in Heaven. Feed us Your Word; feed us Your power; feed us Your substance."*

We need more from God than bread, water, and a diet cola. Physical food and drink are fringe benefits God provides; those are things that man has made (albeit from God's raw materials). But to really *live*, we need the substance of *God*. You need the substance of God, the power of God, and the Spirit of God in order to be more than just a shell of yourself.

If you're going to dominate your domain, then every single day you need to pray, *"Father, give me Your strength. Give me Your power. Help me walk in Your authority. Give me Your strategies and Your creativity. Whatever You're doing up there, do here. You're creating things up there, so create here on earth—and in my life—too. In Heaven You're making things, strategizing, preparing, planning, and working. So I just want You to know, I want You to do in me—and in my life—everything that You're doing up there."*

God can give you a kid's meal or even a ribeye steak if you need it. But if that's all you ask for, you're short-changing Him. The reality is that He is the God of all things. He is the One who makes a way where there is no way. So ask Him for more than just a T-bone! Ask Him for His power. He wants to reveal His glory to you. He wants to reveal His nature to you. In this Kingdom, He wants us to be His likeness on the earth.

Today, to activate this principle, I want you to go somewhere by yourself with God—your car, your house, wherever—and pray for something big. Pray for something that God is doing in Heaven.

Don't pray a little prayer; pray a big prayer.

Ask Him to reveal His glory and nature to you. Ask Him for that ribeye steak, yes; but ask Him for so much more. Ask Him to make your life look just like Heaven.

WHAT IS YOUR BIG PRAYER?

Write it here and keep asking until you receive it.

_____

_____

_____

_____

_____

_____

_____

_____

_____

_____

_____

_____

_____

_____

_____

_____

Date Received: _____

CHAPTER 8

ACTIVATE YOUR DREAM

"For we are His workmanship, created in Christ Jesus for good works, which God prepared beforehand that we should walk in them."
Ephesians 2:10 NKJV

God's Kingdom represents the eternal kingship of God. It is the realm in which God's will is fulfilled. It is actually the realm in which God's dreams are fulfilled—through *you* and *your dreams.*

Are you dreaming anything right now?

I believe you are; I believe you're dreaming something right now. There's something in you that's stirring you; something that's driving you. Your dream has purpose in it. It has flames on it. It's almost like you can't contain yourself, it's so strong.

Jeremiah said, "It's like fire shut up in my bones." I believe you have a dream like that—a vision like that. Do you believe it? Have you activated your dream?

You must understand this:

As a supernatural being in a natural habitat, the dream you're dreaming has already been dreamed. It was dreamed by a sovereign God. He has already dreamed that dream on your behalf; He has already seen the vision that you're seeing right now. He has already strategized it.

That's what the Kingdom of Heaven is about. The Kingdom is God dreaming *there* (in Heaven) so that you can dream *here*. And whenever you dream a thing, you're dreaming what has already happened; because when God dreams a thing, He speaks a thing. And whenever He speaks a thing, it is established. It is created and finished in that moment.

I SO want you to understand that you are a Kingdom person.

God, in His purpose, has always had a plan to bring His Kingdom to the earthly realm. In Genesis 1:1, we read the words, "In the beginning, God..." and we have to look at just those words before we ever go to the next part.

"In the beginning, God."

You must understand that, in His sovereignty, in the beginning—GOD. That's it. His name *is* the whole sentence. In the beginning...GOD.

The word for "God" there in the original Hebrew is *Elohim*. It's plural and refers to the Father, Son, and Holy Spirit. It means that, in the beginning, all three Persons of the Trinity were talking about what was about to happen. It also means that God Himself was the Source of what was about to happen. Everything we see around us started and proceeded forth from this simple truth:

"In the beginning, God."

In the beginning, there was a gathering. God in three Persons gathered together and had a conference call with Himself, if you will. And after that, in the beginning, God created. He created everything out of nothing. He created the heavens and the earth.

It was in the beginning that God made the decision to implement His dream. He made a conscious decision. He said, "We're going to do this, because I want what We have here in Heaven to be there on earth too. The power we demonstrate here in Heaven, with thunder, lightning, and all types of supernatural demonstrations, I want to manifest on earth too."

See, we think it all started to happen when we came to the earth...but no. You and I are just a mirror of what's been going on up there in Heaven for all eternity.

That's why I know that you are dreaming something: because *God* is dreaming something. Because your life on earth is supposed to be a reflection of His life in Heaven. And because your life *is* the dream He has held since eternity past.

Your assignment today is to yield yourself to God for the releasing of His dream on earth.

So, stop what you're doing right now and give yourself over to Him as a tool in His hand to release His dreams through your life.

The dreams you thought you came up with are really the dreams He already conceived a long time ago. So tell Him either all over again or for the very first time that He can dream His dreams and do His work through you today.

CHAPTER 9

WALK IN YOUR DOMINION

"For God has not given us a spirit of fear, but of power and of love and of a sound mind."
2 Timothy 1:7 NKJV

When God made people, He made us in His image. Then, in Genesis 1, we read that He went on to assign us DOMINION.

Genesis 1:26-28 says:

> *"Then God said, 'Let Us make man in Our image, according to Our likeness; let them have dominion over the fish of the sea, over the birds of the air, and over the cattle, over all the earth and over every creeping thing that creeps on the earth.' So God created man in His own image; in the image of God He created him; male and female He created them. Then God blessed them, and God said to them, 'Be fruitful and multiply; fill the earth and subdue it; have dominion over the fish of the sea, over the birds of the air, and over every living thing that moves on the earth'" (NKJV).*

The *opposite* of dominion is being under someone's

control—or even being enslaved. If you don't dominate, you're in subjection to something. So when God said, "Man will have dominion over these things of the earth," He was saying you would be in total control. He was saying that you would not be intimidated by the things of the earth.

Some of you live in craven fear of things on the earth. You live in abject fear of even the natural creatures over which God gave you dominion! You even live in fear of normal life events. But GOD said, "I've given you dominion over the earth. Be fruitful and subdue it."

You need to understand that you are powerful.

Let me restate that:

YOU
NEED TO UNDERSTAND
THAT YOU
ARE POWERFUL.

You have dominion over the earth, and you need to understand the power of your Kingdom calling. You're not passive. You're not a has-been. You're not a mistake or a surprise. You're not a worthless somebody without purpose or cause. Some people may have tried to assign those things to you; but when GOD creates something, He doesn't create trash. He creates treasure.

You are treasure.

When God spoke the words of creation, the Bible simply says: "And it was so." What He spoke happened—no questions asked; no negotiations. His dream happened at His Word, and His Word created and gave you dominion.

Every one of us has places or areas of life in which we are not walking in the dominion God gave us. However, we need to progressively advance in our dominion. We need to get used to walking in dominion and used to carrying God's governmental mantle. We need to strengthen our shoulders to carry the weight and the power of the authority God has granted each one of us through the name and the blood of Jesus Christ.

Today, I want you to think about the places in your life over which you have NOT been exhibiting dominion. Confess these to God and ask Him to help you walk in the authority He has given you.

Also, confess your fears to God today. Ask Him to fill you with perfect love, which casts out fear. Confess out loud that God has not given you a spirit of fear, but of power, love, and a sound mind. Then ask God to instill in you His Kingdom aggression so you can carry out His dominion on the earth.

Pray the prayer on the following page, filling in the blanks appropriately:

"Lord, I come to you and confess that I have not been exhibiting dominion in the areas of _____. I ask You boldly to lead me step by step as I now move forward in faith and in Kingdom authority to manifest Heaven on earth. I release the fears I've had about _____ and I thank You that I do NOT have a spirit of fear, but of power, love, and a sound mind. Amen."

CHAPTER 10

EXERCISE YOUR NAMING RIGHTS

"...God, who gives life to the dead and calls those things
which do not exist as though they did."
Romans 4:17b NKJV

When God created Adam, He formed Adam out of the dirt. He blew His own breath into Adam's nostrils and gave him his Kingdom assignment. But right after that, God gave Adam a job: to NAME all the beasts of the field, the birds of the air, and even the Adam's helpmate, the woman, that God had made.

At that point in the creation story, God was in Adam's domain. Adam had already been given dominion in the land. So God told him to fulfill his function as the master over the land by naming the other creatures on the earth. And when Adam named the things, by giving them names *he gave them assignments*. Literally in being named, those creatures *became* what they were supposed to be.

Just like Adam, YOU need to name what YOU see right now. You need to name the dream that God has conceived

for you.

Whatever you're dreaming—the thing God created before eternity past; the thing He put in your spirit to do—YOU need to name it right now. God has given you naming rights, just like He gave Adam. And when you exercise your naming rights, your dream will become what it's supposed to be.

You've been afraid to name it...because you've been convinced you can't have it.

But you can.

The Bible says to call into existence those things that be not as though they are. The Bible says that whatever you call it, it shall be. Why? Because God has given you the dominion and the naming-right authority to command that thing to BE—to come into existence.

This is why it's so important to name your seed when you sow an offering. This is why you have to confess your dream out loud to God...because if you don't name your gifting, if you don't name your seed offering, it won't become what it's supposed to be.

But I have dominion in the land. YOU have dominion in the land. And if I have dominion in the land, I can speak to everything I want to exist—and it will come. So can you.

Some of you are going to think that's flighty faith—but it's not. That's the Word. God gives you naming rights just like He gave Adam. And whatever GOD created that He wants to birth on the earth, you can name and see it become what it's supposed to be.

So what is your dream?

Speak it out today; call it by name!

Is it your dream to be married? Speak it out:

"Lord, I'm naming my dream. My dream is my marriage, God—my happy, healthy, divinely-appointed marriage to the Kingdom spouse YOU have chosen for me!"

Is your dream to be wealthy and prosperous? Speak it out; name your life!

"God, my dream is my wealth and prosperity—the wealth and prosperity that You created for me before the foundation of the world! I name my life right now: that I am debt-free, healthy, wealthy; I am the owner of a prosperous business; and I walk in total health, wisdom, and abundance in all areas!"

Whatever *your* dream is, name your dream right now. Name your vision. Speak out and write down EXACTLY what the things are that God has put in your heart. You have dominion over those things, so call them forth by their names today.

NAME YOUR DREAM HERE:

_____

_____

_____

_____

_____

_____

_____

_____

_____

_____

_____

_____

_____

_____

_____

CHAPTER 11

RENOVATE YOUR MINDSET

*"And do not be conformed to this world, but be transformed
by the renewing of your mind, that you may prove what is
that good and acceptable
and perfect will of God."*
Romans 12:2 NKJV

I feel that there's a "coming home" happening among God's people. There's a merging; we're merging now more than ever before with the Kingdom purposes of God; with the thoughts of His Spirit. We are forcefully advancing to take the territory away from the kingdom of darkness and return it to God. And the stronger we get in God, the more powerful the manifestation of His Kingdom is going to be.

We serve a righteous Lord—Jesus Christ—who mends the brokenhearted; who sets the captives free; who delivers you from the lies of the past. That's the Kingdom of God in the earth. Sin is sin, and sin is damned to hell in the kingdom of the world; but in the Kingdom of God there is forgiveness and redemption for all mankind through the blood of Jesus Christ.

To start seeing this in our lives, though, we have to start thinking like God thinks. We have to start thinking *souls*. We have to begin operating like God operates. We have to renew our minds and let God heal our thinking.

As a pastor, my heart is simply to see the sheep flourish. I care so much about your status, your state of mind, and the state of your life. Everybody bears a burden. And I'm not diminishing the burdens of life, but the burden of life are fed by the kingdom of the world.

The heavy burdens of this world—like pain, hurt, failure, and the *"I can't"* type of thinking—are not from the Kingdom of Heaven. The Kingdom of Heaven destroys those things. That's why God's intention is and has always been to bring Heaven to invade the earth.

God's way of thinking is a full blown, thought out, supernatural strategy that the world will not be able to swallow.

But if you will renew your mind in the Word of God, you can carry it out. You can manifest God's Kingdom on the earth.

Ultimately, you're not going to be judged based on how you were raised. You're going to be judged on the authority of God's Word. Our problem in the Body of Christ in general is that:

- We don't know the Word;
- We're not standing on the authority of the Word;
- We're not allowing the Word to shape our lives; and

- We're not raising our children based on the truth of the Word.

Some talk show host's magazine or TV program will not help you raise your children. Wall Street won't help you build your family. The nearest feel-good preacher won't help you transform your mind.

But God's Word will help you establish Heaven on the earth. God's Word will cause you to manifest the Kingdom in your family, in your finances, and in your marriage. God's Word will transform your life by the renewing of your mind, so you can prove what His good, acceptable, and perfect will is on the earth.

The earth is simply a colony of Heaven. God created it that way in the beginning. Then, when it fell, He sent Jesus to set up the colony of Heaven on earth again. Now, through the eternal blood of Jesus Christ, Heaven's colony on this planet is forevermore connected to the King. And whatever is on the King—the government over the colony—gets all over the people in the colony.

If you want to participate in seeing Heaven invade your life, all you have to do is submit yourself to the King's Lordship and rise up to govern in His name. Be not conformed to this world but be transformed instead. Renew your mind. Wash your thinking in the water of the Word. Make God's Word your final authority and obey Him in everything. Start thinking like the citizen of Heaven that you are, and your actions will follow as your mind submits to the King of Heaven.

No matter where you are, stop and commit yourself to the Lord in prayer right now. Commit yourself to be His ambassador on the earth. Decide to release and implement His Heaven onto the earth everywhere you go from now on.

Accept your commission!

Accept your Kingdom assignment to ADVANCE—and ask the Lord to spur you on, never letting you become lax in your Kingdom aggression from this time forth and forevermore.

PART 3

COMMISSIONED TO HOLINESS

INTRODUCTION

"Therefore submit to God. Resist the devil and he will flee from you. Draw near to God and He will draw near to you. Cleanse your hands, you sinners; and purify your hearts, you double-minded."
James 4:7-8

One of the greatest promises in all of Scripture is that the devil will flee from us. When this verse says that the devil will run away from you when you resist him, it means he will scoot away like a dog with his tail between his legs.

When the enemy runs, he runs in terror. When you resist him, he flees from you and runs away in abject terror.

However, there's a prerequisite: you have to submit yourself to God first. It's actually the act of submitting to God that empowers you to resist the devil. It all starts with submitting to God.

We have to remember that we are saved by God's grace. We're washed in His mercy.

We're cleansed by the blood of Jesus, and we can't do anything until we recognize that we are totally dependent on God.

In the original Greek, that word for "submit" (in the phrase "submit to God") means:

- to be subordinate to authority;

- to be in obedience and in an attitude of obedience;

- to be submissive;

- to be under subjection.

If you have an attitude of total submission to the Lord, then the devil is going to flee from you. But, he's not going to flee from you if you don't already have these other things in place.

Your attitude of submission actually makes you strong, not weak. When we submit to authority, we become empowered.

Next, if you take the word "resist" and look at it in the original Greek, it means to be a "blocker." It literally means:

- vigorously opposing;

- bravely resisting; and

- standing face-to-face against an adversary.

The authority that we gain when we submit to God gives us the right to stand in the face of our attacker, the devil. The authority which we get from God empowers us to block our accuser, the opposition. Just as an antihistamine puts a block on histamine, this word "resist" tells us that, with the authority and spiritual weapons granted to us, we can withstand the evil forces that the enemy brings against us.

How do we do this? By exercising five crucial keys.

1) Be ruled by the Word of God.

2) Beware of grieving the Holy Spirit.

3) Work hard toward wisdom.

4) Resist the first stirring of temptation.

5) Work hard and labor to be filled with the Spirit.

The following chapters in this section will each cover a key on how to resist your enemy. Hear me well as you read these: you can live absolutely outside the enemy's grasp at all times. These keys work, for they are the Word of God.

But, you have to work the keys in order for them to work.

Are you ready to power up? Are you ready to put action to your faith? Here we go!

CHAPTER 12

BE RULED BY
THE WORD OF GOD

"The law of the Lord is perfect, converting the soul; the testimony of the Lord is sure, making wise the simple; the statutes of the Lord are right, rejoicing the heart; the commandment of the Lord is pure, enlightening the eyes; the fear of the Lord is clean, enduring forever; the judgments of the Lord are true and righteous altogether.

More to be desired are they than gold, yea, than much fine gold; sweeter also than honey and the honeycomb.

Moreover by them Your servant is warned, and in keeping them there is great reward."
Psalm 19:7-11

The first key that will keep you out of the grasp of the enemy is to **be ruled by the Word**. The Word of God—the Bible—is our final authority. Make the Word of God your rule and your authority, and live in obedience to all it says.

We teach this every week at the church I pastor—*Dwelling Place Church International*. We teach that if you're not under the authority of the Word, then you're out from under any covering at all. The Word is our final authority, our starting authority, and every authority in between.

It doesn't matter how elementary your life situation may be; always run to the Word. Run to what "Thus says the Lord," because His instruction is steadfast. It will never fail you! And as our final authority, the Word will keep you walking on a straight path. It will guard you from all manner of temptation.

When I do premarital counseling, I always teach future brides and grooms to keep the Word in the middle of your marriage relationship. If you keep God in the center of your life and your everyday living, then every foul word, any obstacle, anything that comes up, goes through the filter of God's Word first. If God is in the middle of your relationship, you automatically start changing the way you think and act to align with the Bible.

Keep the Word in the middle of your life and in everything that you do. Let every aspect of your life be based upon and filtered through the reality of this Word.

CHAPTER 13

BEWARE OF GRIEVING THE HOLY SPIRIT

"Do not quench the Spirit."
1 Thessalonians 5:19

If you want to live outside the grasp of the enemy, then always ***beware of grieving the Holy Spirit.***

When I say, "Beware of grieving the Holy Spirit," I mean don't offend the Spirit.

A lot of the time, people freak out and get afraid they have permanently grieved the Holy Spirit. They say, "No, no, no, I've offended the Holy Spirit. I've gone too far. I've committed the unpardonable sin. I've done all of that."

But, it's actually harder to commit the unpardonable sin than you realize because the unpardonable sin is to completely turn your back on the belief system of God and say, "He doesn't exist." That's not what we mean when we talk about not quenching the Holy Spirit.

"Quenching the Holy Spirit" means, for example:

- Shutting Him down whenever He's moving;

- Offending Him by carrying an attitude that's not aligned with Scripture; or

- Doing an activity that's not according to Scripture.

We have to be careful and aware of the Holy Spirit so that we don't grieve Him. He has feelings, and He is a PERSON—not an "it." (I'll just throw that in.)

The Holy Spirit is the one who gives us as Christians the ability to discern Satan's temptations.

Do you know what conviction is? It starts with the Convicter—the Holy Spirit. He is the person of the Trinity who is going to make sure that you say, "Oh, I better not do that. I better not go in there. I better not watch that show. I better not drink that. I better not, I better not, I better not." He is the one who convicts us, and He does so in compassion and in love. He's the one who is going to bring that sense of discernment to us, so we can say, "Oh, I recognize this trap. I recognize what the enemy is trying to do."

The Holy Spirit has an assignment to help you discern and recognize when the enemy is attacking you, tripping you up, or leading you down a path. The Holy Spirit helps you fend off enemy attacks. If you listen to the Holy Spirit in your life, combining your discernment with the authority of God's Word, the Lord will protect you from the enemy's grasp. He'll give you grace and show you how to navigate through life.

The Spirit is always at work to do the good pleasure of the Father. He's always with you, helping you. He doesn't take a day off. He is always protecting us from satanic attacks.

CHAPTER 14

WORK HARD
TOWARD WISDOM

"At Gibeon the Lord appeared to Solomon in a dream by night; and God said, "Ask! What shall I give you?"

And Solomon said: "You have shown great mercy to Your servant David my father, because he walked before You in truth, in righteousness, and in uprightness of heart with You; You have continued this great kindness for him, and You have given him a son to sit on his throne, as it is this day. Now, O Lord my God, You have made Your servant king instead of my father David, but I am a little child; I do not know how to go out or come in.

And Your servant is in the midst of Your people whom You have chosen, a great people, too numerous to be numbered or counted. Therefore give to Your servant an understanding heart to judge Your people, that I may discern between good and evil. For who is able to judge this great people of Yours?"

The speech pleased the Lord, that Solomon had asked this thing. Then God said to him: "Because you have asked this

thing, and have not asked long life for yourself, nor have
asked riches for yourself, nor have asked the life of your
enemies, but have asked for yourself understanding to
discern justice, behold, I have done according to your
words; see, I have given you a wise and understanding
heart, so that there has not been anyone like you before you,
nor shall any like you arise after you.

And I have also given you what you have not asked: both
riches and honor, so that there shall not be anyone like you
among the kings all your days. So if you walk in My ways,
to keep My statutes and My commandments, as your father
David walked, then I will
lengthen your days."
1 Kings 3:5-14

To live outside the grasp of the devil, we need to **labor or work hard toward wisdom.**

In the passage above, Solomon's attitude was, "I don't need all of the stuff. I just need wisdom. I know that, more than anything, I'm going to need the wisdom of heaven. I'm going to need the knowledge of heaven; and yet, wisdom is of the utmost importance."

There is a great difference between knowledge and wisdom. "Knowledge" pertains to accumulating the facts, but applying Scripture to those facts means they can become wisdom.

It is not the Christian with the most knowledge who is best equipped to battle the enemy's temptations. *Instead, it is the Christian with the most wisdom who is equipped to battle*

Satan's temptations.

You can have every Sunday School lapel pin that exists, but still not have wisdom. You can be a regular churchgoer who never misses a Sunday at church—but still not have wisdom. You can have plenty of knowledge, but still not have wisdom.

The wisdom of God gives you discernment and the ability to recognize things in the Spirit realm. Someone who is well-versed in discernment and wisdom can walk into a room and smell any demons that are there.

I think Solomon understood this, or he would have never asked God for wisdom. He told God, "I want Your wisdom. Above all else, I want Your wisdom." Then, God said, "Okay, since you asked for wisdom, I'm going to give you everything that you desire in your heart. I'm going to give you all of it simply because you put Me before yourself; because you asked for My wisdom." And the Bible tells us that, like Solomon, we can actually possess the wisdom of the Creator of all things. We just have to be willing to pursue it and work toward it.

My grandmother and grandfather were extremely wise Christians. Whenever you look at a family that raises children who are all in the Lord, there is always a godly foundation of wisdom in that family. It doesn't mean there wasn't any struggle. It doesn't mean there wasn't any failure. It doesn't mean there weren't any mishaps. But, in those families you will find a cord of wisdom throughout the family's generational line.

The cord of God's wisdom exists generationally.

That's why it's so important that we sit under the auspices of godly teaching and godly knowledge. It's never too early to start developing godly wisdom. We need to start asking God for wisdom wherever we are, so that we can create a cord that exists from generation to generation. Establishing generational godly wisdom is a big part of how you resist the devil.

When my wife, Pastor Judy Jacobs Tuttle, was young, her dad would get up early in the morning on their farm. He would get up even earlier than chore time because he had to pray for all of his children and his grandchildren. He would go up into the top of the barn, and his family could hear him praying all the way in the house. He would lift up his voice and call out every name: the names of the daughters and sons, their wives and husbands, and even every child. My wife even remembers listening to hear her daddy call her name in prayer. That's the heritage of prayer and godly wisdom!

Not everybody has a story of generational wisdom, and I respect that. I'm not downgrading anybody's story. However, the reality is that you can start building future generations for good right now. You can start your own thread of wisdom in your household, setting a new standard going forward. Go ahead and break the curse! Break the old mindset. Break the idea that says, "This is the way it's always been, so this is the way it's always going to be. I'm always going to be a victim; my dad was this and my mom was that." Break that thinking off yourself right now!

My life hasn't been a perfect walk. But I learned far enough in advance that my mom and dad knew something that I didn't know. Their secret had to do with righteous living—righteous living made possible by godly wisdom. And their wisdom passed generationally has made all the difference in my generation and in the lives of my children as well.

CHAPTER 15

RESIST THE FIRST STIRRING OF TEMPTATION

"Therefore let him who thinks he stands take heed lest he fall. No temptation has overtaken you except such as is common to man; but God is faithful, who will not allow you to be tempted beyond what you are able, but with the temptation will also make the way of escape, that you may be able to bear it."
1 Corinthians 10:12-13

No one is exempt from temptation. How do we know this? Because Jesus was in all manner tempted as we are, and yet he didn't sin. Therefore, none of us is an exception to the rule: you WILL be tempted.

When we're tempted, however, we have to **resist the first stirring of temptation**. It doesn't matter where you're standing or what you're doing. This applies to everybody—every age, every demographic, every Christian, no matter how mature or immature. We all have to resist the first stirring of temptation. You have to resist the first stirring of temptation. We all do.

It is safe to resist temptation, but it's dangerous to dabble in temptation.

Can I share a testimony?

When I was about eighteen years old, I was already a Christian. I had been raised in a Christian home. I was playing music by the time I was six or seven years old; we were traveling on a bus to minister and all of that. But as I got older, I wanted to explore.

Now, before I go further, let me say this: I'm not giving anybody permission to go explore by sharing this testimony. But, I am sharing this because I want you to see how dangerous it is to dabble in temptation. So here's what happened:

Because I was eighteen, and I was so rhythmic, I wanted to go "shake my groove thing." I wanted to go to the club. I didn't want to go to the club to drink; I wanted to go to dance. I really liked to dance, and I could throw it down.

So, I went down at a club in Myrtle Beach. They knew me by name at that club because I was going in every night. That last day, the song ended and I walked off the dance floor. I just had dabbled in temptation; that was all. But as I walked off the dance floor, there was a young man from my home church. The only thing he knew about me was that I am the son of Don and Parmalee Tuttle and that I played the drums for their Gospel music group. He had never seen me in any other environment or anything.

Well, I saw that man watching me on the dance floor. And

when I came off the floor, he said to me, "I cannot believe I am seeing you in this club. I will never be able to see you any differently than how I've seen you tonight."

I did what I could to fix things with that man that night, and I have never gone "clubbing" since. Nevertheless, I have never lived that down, even all these years later. This just goes to show that it's better to resist temptation than to deal with the danger of dabbling in it.

I heard Jentezen Franklin preach a message about this once. He said, "You've got thirty seconds. You have a timeframe of thirty seconds to deny the temptation, because in thirty seconds your mind will change. No matter what the temptation is, if you can adjust your thought process within those thirty seconds, then you overcome the temptation."

We've got to resist temptation. God's Word promises that we can resist temptation; it doesn't say that we can resist sin once we begin dabbling in that temptation. So actually, the dabbling leads to the action.

You may be thinking:

- *"I'm strong enough. I'm just witnessing to him."*
- *"No, I'm just going to take her out. I know her story."*
- *"I'm going to try this."*

And the biggie right now:

- *"We don't get drunk. We just do the social thing."*

If you're thinking any of those things, or even similar things, you're stepping into a dabbling moment. You're on dangerous ground. Ultimately, the enemy has a big trap set for you. Stop dabbling in temptation and start resisting it at its first stirrings.

CHAPTER 16

WORK HARD AND LABOR TO BE FILLED WITH THE SPIRIT

"And do not be drunk with wine, in which is dissipation; but be filled with the Spirit"
Ephesians 5:18

Your giftings, your talents, and the things that you do so well have nothing to do with you. They have to do with the Spirit of God, the power of God, and the gifting of God that He has given you.

Your life can be filled with power only if you are filled with the Holy Spirit. I know a lot of talented people who have no power because they don't know the Holy Spirit. We always need the Spirit—so we **labor diligently and discipline ourselves to stay filled with the Spirit.**

Imagine that your life is a chair. That chair only has room for one person to sit in it. And in the Spirit realm, either God can sit in that chair or the devil can. You can't have both.

There is a fight for position in your life. Jesus said, "You can't serve both. You can't be in the world and in the Kingdom." You always have to make a choice. The person who will sit in the chair of your life is either going to be the devil or the Holy Spirit, so you have to make up your mind.

Always remember that YOU are the one who makes up your mind. YOU are the one who decides who will sit enthroned on your life. And the enemy never plays fair, so it takes effort to fight the good fight of faith.

If you want to live outside the grasp of the enemy, you have to work hard to be *and stay* FILLED with the Holy Spirit. I'm not just talking about a one-time experience, in which you're filled with the Spirit and the evidence of speaking in tongues. I'm talking about a lifestyle of being filled with the Spirit. That's a lifestyle in which God is enthroned on the chair of your life, and there is a fight for that position going on right now. There will always be a fight for that position.

There is a fight for the throne of your life. You have to work hard to win it for God.

You have to be faithful and diligent to let the Holy Spirit rule your life. You have to be faithful and diligent to bear godly fruit. You have to practice submitting to God and resisting the devil.

To live outside the grasp of the enemy, we all have to fight through learning, working, and practicing the things of God. We have to practice and labor to obey God and yield to His Lordship. We must be diligent to obey James 4:10: "Humble yourselves in the sight of the Lord, and He will lift you up."

I pray a keeping grace over you right now as you read this. I believe that your heart and motives are pure, and you're submitting to God—but that doesn't necessarily mean that resisting is easy. So, I release the ability of God into you to resist temptation and resist dabbling in it. I release the ability of God to even resist worry, because the Bible calls worrying a sin. Every good and perfect gift comes from the Father of lights, and He wants to take care of His own. He is going to take care of you and keep you with His keeping grace.

The Lord has a plan in place for your life. He knows from one day to the next exactly how that plan unfolds. Don't give into the temptation of fear, doubt, and unbelief. Stand strong in faith, and be filled with the Holy Spirit. Be diligent and work hard to always be led by the Spirit of God. Labor to make His Word your reality and final authority in everything.

Stop and speak your praise to God right now. This is a turning point for some of you. I believe that these five keys represent a turning point for you. And right now, I believe the Holy Spirit is making all these keys click for you like a key in a keyhole. Right now, things are coming into light and understanding in your spirit. You don't have to fear and fret. You don't have to worry. Your Father God never causes you to worry. No, He's your Father who gives you victory. He gives you the calm assurance of knowing that He is God, no matter the situation.

So resist the devil.

Resist the very thought of failure. Resist the very thought of the enemy destroying anything. Resist the very thought that you're going to lose it all or that you can't be healed. Resist the thought that you can't be successful. Submit all those thoughts to the Word of God, which is our final authority—and let the Word expose those things as the lies they are.

You and I are children of God—the Most High God. Failing is not in our vocabulary. Failing is not in our DNA. Instead, being a success is in our DNA.

Being righteous means to be right; to be in right standing with God himself. If you're in sin or if you've even been dabbling in temptation, confess to the Lord right now. Just pray this to the Lord:

> *"Lord, I repent. I confess. Lord, I repent even before I finish reading this book. I repent for dabbling. I repent for not believing. I repent for thinking that certain things are okay, when I know in my heart of hearts that You're not pleased with certain things. I put it on the altar right now, and I ask You to forgive me. Fill me with Your Holy Spirit, and make me new with the blood of Your Son Jesus."*

Nothing the enemy could ever offer you is worth giving up God's blessings for. Christ came to give you life, and life abundantly. His life is better than anything on the earth.

So resist the devil. Resist temptation. Stand for righteousness. Choose to be different by the power of the Holy Spirit. Live consecrated to God, and you will live outside the enemy's grasp.

PART 4

COMMISSIONED INTO REVIVAL

CHAPTER 17

PREPARE FOR RAIN AND GOLD

"Then Elijah said to Ahab, 'Go up, eat and drink; for there is the sound of abundance of rain.' So Ahab went up to eat and drink. And Elijah went up to the top of Carmel; then he bowed down on the ground, and put his face between his knees, and said to his servant, 'Go up now, look toward the sea.'

So he went up and looked, and said, 'There is nothing.' And seven times he said, 'Go again.'

Then it came to pass the seventh time, that he said, 'There is a cloud, as small as a man's hand, rising out of the sea!' So he said, 'Go up, say to Ahab, 'Prepare your chariot, and go down before the rain stops you.''

Now it happened in the meantime that the sky became black with clouds and wind, and there was a heavy rain. So Ahab rode away and went to Jezreel. Then the hand of the Lord came upon Elijah; and he girded up his loins and ran ahead of Ahab to the entrance of Jezreel."

1 Kings 18:41-45

I had a dream recently in which I was on the platform with Pastor Rod Parsley, my friend, who is the pastor and founder of *World Harvest Church*, as well as the leader of *City Harvest Network*, of which my church is a part. In this dream, Pastor Parsley was preaching and my church members were in the congregation. Suddenly, Pastor Parsley turned to me and said, "What has happened in your life?"

In that moment, the dream shifted from Pastor Parsley preaching to my standing up and telling an actual testimony from my past.

In this dream, I stood up and told the story of how, about 20 years ago, I had been saving money for a pickup truck. After a year of saving, I had $9,000. However, instead of letting me purchase a truck with that money, the Lord told me to sow it into the evangelism efforts of a church where we were the visiting ministers. Just days later, someone I didn't know gave me a brand- new, GOLD Ford Ranger—the exact kind of truck I wanted. I still have it to this day.

Still in the dream, after I told this story on the platform with Pastor Parsley, he looked at me and said, "You still have the truck— and its color represents the next outpouring." At that, I woke up, and the Lord spoke to me and said, "Get ready for rain. Get ready for gold," and He said that this word is for everyone who will take it.

As I began to study this word, the Lord took me to the passage in 1 Kings above and showed me several things.

1. **Elijah understood that, in order for a spiritual manifestation to happen in the natural, there had to be consecration.**

The prophet Elijah could do a lot of things under the anointing, but he recognized that certain things wouldn't happen without in- depth prayer. Elijah knew the condition of Israel. Israel was a mess. It had turned away from God and was worshipping idols. Nevertheless, God never lost His desire to pour out His blessing.

Similarly, we're in a position right now as the Body of Christ where we have to make a very, *very* important decision. That decision is this: Are we okay with the status quo? Do we want dry religion? Or, are we going to pray for rain? Are we willing to put our head between our knees and intercede?

If you haven't already, I urge you to sanctify yourself and enter a season of consecration, fasting, and prayer. The spiritual season we are in is laden with promise, but none of God's promises will come forth without consecration, fasting, and prayer.

2. **Elijah dared his servant over and over again to go look for that cloud.**

Seven times, Elijah told his servant to go look for rain. Elijah was a prophet in the land and he felt the urgency of his prayers. He knew, "If I don't pray, rain's not coming..." and that's the way we have to be as the Body of Christ. If we're not praying, rain is not coming.

The only thing that makes rain is consecration. The thing that brings those rain clouds is getting before the Lord and saying, "God, it doesn't matter what happens. It doesn't matter who's doing what. We want rain." Even if we have to go look for the rain seven times, we still have to stay in that position of dependence on God. We can't say that we've been planting seed for six months, six years, or six days and then get tired and think that's good enough. No, six is the number of man— but breakthrough came at SEVEN, the number of God. Breakthrough did not come at six!

God is not going to show up with your miracle on the sixth time. Men would try to get credit for it if He did. But the word of the Lord for you today is that you must endure until the seventh time comes! If you can endure until the seventh time comes, then you know God will do it and He'll get all the credit.

3. **When the seventh time comes, you'll see something you've never seen before.**

On his seventh time of checking for rain, the servant ran back to the prophet and said, "I see a cloud the size of a man's hand." That servant didn't see much; he only saw a tiny cloud. But you know what? You don't need to see a monstrous hurricane. You just need to see that God is about to step in. You only need to know that one thing is rising up and something else is falling down.

I speak this prophetically over you right now: Your last season is falling down and your rain is rising up. And in this new season, you're going to need buckets and an umbrella! You're going to need something to protect you from the sheer force of this mighty outpouring, and you're going to need something to catch it with at the same time.

4.   God is on the move, and His work is not a man's idea.

There are two types of rain coming: rain on the earth and rain for people individually. Rain and gold are going to fall into your life if you will consecrate yourself. But, even more importantly than that, fire will fall also.

On the day when Elijah defeated the prophets of Baal, it wasn't the rain that defeated them. It was the fire of God that caused Israel to cry out, *"The Lord, He is God! The Lord, He is God!"* (1 Kings 18:39). I don't know about you, but I want fire that burns the altars of Baal. I want fire that destroys the agenda of Baal. Do you?

5.   When revival fire hits, rain and gold always fall.

When the Lord sends revival fire, He sends plenty of everything:

- Salvation for your lost family members
- Restoration for your marriage
- Plenty of money
- Plenty of opportunity
- Plenty of jobs for people who need them, and more.

6.   When revival hits, everything comes into alignment with the move of God.

Some people want to be millionaires or billionaires, and there's nothing wrong with that if God has called you to it. But we need to want FIRE. We need to put our head between our knees and cry out to the Lord, asking Him to make us Holy Ghost-filled, fire-baptized, dead-raising, tongue-talking, miracle-working men and women who are blazing lights for God.

Do you want the fire of the Holy Spirit? Do you want the great outpouring? You may only be one person, but you can have the rain and the gold. Hear me well: *The size of your cloud will never determine the abundance of your rain.*

7. The size of your cloud doesn't determine the abundance of rain.

You may feel all alone or like you can't make much of a difference. But I'm telling you today that "Little is much when God is in it." Elijah's servant said, "I saw a cloud coming up from the depths of the sea. It's the size of a man's hand." And at that, the prophet had heard enough. He got up; the king got in his chariot; and the hand of the Lord came upon Elijah and he ran all the way to Jezreel. All he needed to know was that the Lord was on the way.

8. It's time for us to put our head between our knees and consecrate ourselves until we see the cloud.

Can you draw nigh to Him right now? Rain and gold are coming. Believe God that this is the year of plenty in which you will have the best of both worlds—the spiritual world and the practical world. You will have plenty of revelation and plenty of revenue.

But, if you want to participate, you have to prepare for rain. Put your buckets out. Get your umbrella ready. The rain and the gold are going to come down on everybody who wants them.

So position yourself, stay in focus, remain confident of everything God has called you to be, and POWER UP! This is going to be good.

ABOUT THE AUTHOR

Jamie Tuttle serves as Lead Pastor of *Dwelling Place Church International* in Cleveland, Tennessee. Born in Winston Salem, North Carolina, he was raised in a music evangelism family. He began playing drums at the age of five, which opened many doors for him and ultimately led him to Cleveland, Tennessee. He holds a Master of Divinity degree with an emphasis on Marriage and Family.

In 1993, he married Pastor Judy Jacobs. Together they began ministering around the world through their ministry, *His Song Ministries* (HSM). In addition to leading *Dwelling Place Church International*, Pastor Jamie also serves as CEO of HSM, which includes *Judy Jacobs International*, *His Song Music Group*, *Dwelling Room Studios*, and the *International Institute of Mentoring*. Pastors Jamie and Judy have two daughters, Kaylee and Erica.